Food
for
Thought
JOURNAL

OUR FAMILY'S
RECIPES FOR WISDOM

Nick Foulks

INTRODUCTION

*Excerpt from Food for Thought: 20 Life Lessons
from a Southern Black Mother*

"Growing up as a black kid in a primarily white area I felt a lot like a zebra sometimes. I was black but painted with white mannerisms and characteristics. Even though I was surrounded by white culture I was not fully accepted. As I got older and ventured into the inner city to play high level basketball and found myself yet again on the outside looking in at a culture that said I didn't quite fit. It seemed even harder there, in the black culture, where I desired to be accepted. That desire for acceptance was strong but what was even stronger were the words and teachings of my family. Teachings that I learned crossed racial and cultural barriers because they were simply the realities of life. And these realities came into play whether you are dealing with white people, black people, brown people, or purple people eaters. It speaks to us all in some fashion."

We call it *Food for Thought*. The full expression would go something like this: "Baby, this is food for thought, take out of it what you need. Eat the meat and spit out the bones." Meaning, you may not agree with everything I'm about to say, but if there is something in it that can help you, then grab hold of it.

Over the years my mom gave me a lot of meat to chew on, if you will. She was from the south and you may not know this, but people from the south have a lot of sayings. Nuggets of truth that sometimes punch you in the gut and others that simply soothe the soul.

Many of these life lessons honestly have saved my life. They have given me peace, strength, hope, and courage. I hope they do the same for you. But again—take out of this what you need. It's just *Food for Thought.*

For the full stories behind Mama Foulks' proverbs, read: *Food for Thought: 20 Life Lessons from a Southern Black Mother.*

If you haven't had the opportunity to read the book I encourage you to purchase your copy at nickfoulks.com or anywhere books are sold.

This journal comes in two sections, a section to journal about the lessons I have learned and passed on to you, and a second section, perhaps even more meaningful to you, where you can capture your own family's sayings and wisdom for posterity: your children will thank you, but your great grandchildren will treasure it.

SECTION ONE

LESSON 1

"Don't start off today smelling like yesterday."

How many days have you gone forth smelling like the drama of a past day?

What did it cost you?

What is it costing you?

What if you have the power to change? To wash yourself in thoughts of love and thankfulness—to smell like hope rather than hate?

Remember: *You* do *have the power to change.*

LESSON 2

"A steel tongue carries a level head."

REFLECTION

Where do you let your emotions run the conversation?

What would change in your world if you put this into practice?

How would you speak to others if you truly understood the weight of your words?

What have you paid the price for because you let your tongue run wild?

LESSON 3

"Put down that Cinderella shoe."

REFLECTION

Whose "shoes" are you wearing in life?

What causes you to do that?

What would change for you if you put that Cinderella shoe down?

LESSON 4

"Lips weren't meant to go that far down."

REFLECTION

Where in life might you fear creating healthy boundaries?

What is that lack of boundaries costing you?

Whose ass do you need to stop kissing?

LESSON 5

"Learn to live life with an open hand."

REFLECTION

In what area of life might your hands be closed?

How would you feel if you were to release your grip?

What emotions come up when you think about it?

What needs to happen for you to release those areas?

What do you hope to happen if you do?

LESSON 6

"When the heat wears off that's when the love has to kick in."

REFLECTION

When in your life did you let the heat distract you from the heart of a person?

Have you ever felt like when the heat wore off in a relationship everything changed for you? What changed?

How are you moving from heat to heart in your current relationship?

Where do you need the love to kick in right now?

How can you invite your partner into that conversation?

LESSON 7

"It's tongue and teeth, baby, and it's all in there together."

REFLECTION

What tongue-and-teeth moments are showing up in your relationship?

How might things change if you stepped back and assumed the painful inter-action was not on purpose?

How can you be more conscientious with your partner?

LESSON 8

"Baby, you need to learn how to give your own self a shine."

REFLECTION

What are a few things you have accomplished that YOU are proud of?

What would it mean to you to celebrate your journey?

How do you feel when you reflect on where you've been and what you've achieved?

LESSON 9

"Baby, you have to learn to follow your first mind because your first mind is often your right mind."

REFLECTION

What are some times in your life where you have failed to follow your first mind?

What decisions are in front of you now that require you to turn down the volume of imposing thoughts?

What do you feel the greater wisdom inside of you leading you to do in those areas?

How can you make space for stillness and meditation in your own life?

LESSON 10

"Love is what it does, not what it says."

REFLECTION

What relationships in our lives currently exchange the words, "I love you?"

How are we showing up for others we say we love? How are they showing up for us?

What actions do we observe that illustrate the love someone has for us?

What actions can we take to show them love?

LESSON 11

"Call a spade, a spade."

REFLECTION

Where in your life do you need to acknowledge reality?

Where have you played it safe or avoided the potential pain that comes from calling it like it is?

What would change if you started calling a spade a spade in your life?

LESSON 12

"Baby, sometimes people can be crying with a loaf of bread under their arms."

REFLECTION

What is a loaf of bread you are carrying underneath your arms that should allow you to rejoice in this moment, regardless of your circumstances?

Where can you stop allowing complaining to influence your perception?

How might life shift if you take a moment before complaining and recognize the beauty (loaf of bread) in your life?

LESSON 13

"You have to learn to feed people with a long handle spoon."

REFLECTION

Who in your life needs to be fed from a "long handle spoon?"

How have you currently been engaging with these individuals?

How have you felt using the method you are taking?

What would change if you created better boundaries?

What could those boundaries look like?

What emotions do you feel at the thought of implementing those boundaries?

LESSON 14

"If you find a snake in the grass you don't bring it in the house to bite you. Leave that shit where you found it."

REFLECTION

Who have you encountered in the past that turned out to be a "snake?"

What signs did you see in advance that could have prevented the pain you endured?

What, if any, relationships in your life have shown signs of potential snake-like behavior?

What behaviors have you identified in those individuals?

If their actions were to impact you in the way they have impacted others, how would you feel knowing you saw the tendency in advance?

What, if any, decisions should you make or precautions should you take?

LESSON 15

"There is pride and then there is foolish pride."

REFLECTION

Where have you allowed pride to stop you from being vulnerable?

Who can you safely invite into what you are going through?

How would you feel if you knew others cared and wanted to come alongside you?

What, if anything, would stop you from inviting them in?

How could professional help provide additional support to you in this season?

LESSON 16

"Baby, God promises daily bread, not a freezer-full."

REFLECTION

What would change if you took time to give thanks for the ongoing provision you have in your life?

What would change if your focus shifted from more to more grateful for where you are now?

How can you create a practice of gratitude for what you currently have?

LESSON 17

"If you keep sweeping shit under the rug it's gonna come out the other side."

REFLECTION

When you think about the relationships in your life, in what areas might you be sweeping things under the rug?

For what reason do you find yourself doing this?

How might it be coming out the other side?

What might be a healthy manner for sharing your thoughts, frustration, or opinions surrounding these areas?

LESSON 18

"Baby, sometimes you need to just have yourself a good ass cry."

REFLECTION

When can you remember allowing yourself to have a good ass cry?

What were the circumstances that brought you to that point?

What area of your life right now do you need to acknowledge the emotional exhaustion you may be feeling?

How can you make space to allow yourself the emotional release you deserve?

LESSON 19

"Baby, if you do right, then right will follow you."

REFLECTION

What are times in your life where you choose the right thing in light of personal sacrifice?

What happened after you made those decisions?

When have you failed to choose the right thing, but instead chose what you wanted?

What was the result?

What was the difference between those two situations?

What could empower you to choose right each time?

CHAPTER 20

"You hold the power of the pen."

REFLECTION

Where in your life have you seen a change in your life script?

How did you respond when that happened?

Looking back, how have you grown from that change?

Where are you currently seeing a change in your life script?

What would change in your mindset if you took on the power of the pen mentality?

SECTION TWO:

OUR FAMILY'S RECIPES FOR WISDOM

Every family has unique sayings, teachings, or life lessons that are worthy to be passed down from generation to generation. This journal was designed to help capture those lessons so that generations to follow can receive the wisdom of their elders.

Capture those sayings and messages in the journal provided. You can now also turn this into your own book with copies for your family to share, and even include important family photos! Use the QR code below to visit the landing page to work with our partners at Victory Vision Publishing. To publish your own book, you'll have to type your answers into a template, but the journal is a great place to create your draft!

SAYING #1

What is the saying or teaching?

Who shared the saying or teaching? (mom, dad, grandparents, etc.)

Where did it originate?

What is the lesson it teaches?

How has it impacted you personally?

SAYING #2

What is the saying or teaching?

Who shared the saying or teaching? (mom, dad, grandparents, etc.)

Where did it originate?

What is the lesson it teaches?

How has it impacted you personally?

SAYING #3

What is the saying or teaching?

Who shared the saying or teaching? (mom, dad, grandparents, etc.)

Where did it originate?

What is the lesson it teaches?

How has it impacted you personally?

SAYING #4

What is the saying or teaching?

Who shared the saying or teaching? (mom, dad, grandparents, etc.)

Where did it originate?

What is the lesson it teaches?

How has it impacted you personally?

SAYING #5

What is the saying or teaching?

Who shared the saying or teaching? (mom, dad, grandparents, etc.)

Where did it originate?

What is the lesson it teaches?

How has it impacted you personally?

SAYING #6

What is the saying or teaching?

Who shared the saying or teaching? (mom, dad, grandparents, etc.)

Where did it originate?

What is the lesson it teaches?

How has it impacted you personally?

SAYING #7

What is the saying or teaching?

Who shared the saying or teaching? (mom, dad, grandparents, etc.)

Where did it originate?

What is the lesson it teaches?

How has it impacted you personally?

SAYING #8

What is the saying or teaching?

Who shared the saying or teaching? (mom, dad, grandparents, etc.)

Where did it originate?

What is the lesson it teaches?

How has it impacted you personally?

SAYING #9

What is the saying or teaching?

Who shared the saying or teaching? (mom, dad, grandparents, etc.)

Where did it originate?

What is the lesson it teaches?

How has it impacted you personally?

SAYING #10

What is the saying or teaching?

Who shared the saying or teaching? (mom, dad, grandparents, etc.)

Where did it originate?

What is the lesson it teaches?

How has it impacted you personally?

SAYING #11

What is the saying or teaching?

Who shared the saying or teaching? (mom, dad, grandparents, etc.)

Where did it originate?

What is the lesson it teaches?

How has it impacted you personally?

SAYING #12

What is the saying or teaching?

Who shared the saying or teaching? (mom, dad, grandparents, etc.)

Where did it originate?

What is the lesson it teaches?

How has it impacted you personally?

SAYING #13

What is the saying or teaching?

Who shared the saying or teaching? (mom, dad, grandparents, etc.)

Where did it originate?

What is the lesson it teaches?

How has it impacted you personally?

SAYING #14

What is the saying or teaching?

Who shared the saying or teaching? (mom, dad, grandparents, etc.)

Where did it originate?

What is the lesson it teaches?

How has it impacted you personally?

SAYING #15

What is the saying or teaching?

Who shared the saying or teaching? (mom, dad, grandparents, etc.)

Where did it originate?

What is the lesson it teaches?

How has it impacted you personally?

SAYING #16

What is the saying or teaching?

Who shared the saying or teaching? (mom, dad, grandparents, etc.)

Where did it originate?

What is the lesson it teaches?

How has it impacted you personally?

SAYING #17

What is the saying or teaching?

Who shared the saying or teaching? (mom, dad, grandparents, etc.)

Where did it originate?

What is the lesson it teaches?

How has it impacted you personally?

SAYING #18

What is the saying or teaching?

Who shared the saying or teaching? (mom, dad, grandparents, etc.)

Where did it originate?

What is the lesson it teaches?

How has it impacted you personally?

SAYING #19

What is the saying or teaching?

Who shared the saying or teaching? (mom, dad, grandparents, etc.)

Where did it originate?

What is the lesson it teaches?

How has it impacted you personally?

SAYING #20

What is the saying or teaching?

Who shared the saying or teaching? (mom, dad, grandparents, etc.)

Where did it originate?

What is the lesson it teaches?

How has it impacted you personally?

SAYING #21

What is the saying or teaching?

Who shared the saying or teaching? (mom, dad, grandparents, etc.)

Where did it originate?

What is the lesson it teaches?

How has it impacted you personally?

SAYING #22

What is the saying or teaching?

Who shared the saying or teaching? (mom, dad, grandparents, etc.)

Where did it originate?

What is the lesson it teaches?

How has it impacted you personally?

SAYING #23

What is the saying or teaching?

Who shared the saying or teaching? (mom, dad, grandparents, etc.)

Where did it originate?

What is the lesson it teaches?

How has it impacted you personally?

SAYING #24

What is the saying or teaching?

Who shared the saying or teaching? (mom, dad, grandparents, etc.)

Where did it originate?

What is the lesson it teaches?

How has it impacted you personally?

SAYING #25

What is the saying or teaching?

Who shared the saying or teaching? (mom, dad, grandparents, etc.)

Where did it originate?

What is the lesson it teaches?

How has it impacted you personally?

SAYING #26

What is the saying or teaching?

Who shared the saying or teaching? (mom, dad, grandparents, etc.)

Where did it originate?

What is the lesson it teaches?

How has it impacted you personally?

SAYING #27

What is the saying or teaching?

Who shared the saying or teaching? (mom, dad, grandparents, etc.)

Where did it originate?

What is the lesson it teaches?

How has it impacted you personally?

SAYING #28

What is the saying or teaching?

Who shared the saying or teaching? (mom, dad, grandparents, etc.)

Where did it originate?

What is the lesson it teaches?

How has it impacted you personally?

SAYING #29

What is the saying or teaching?

Who shared the saying or teaching? (mom, dad, grandparents, etc.)

Where did it originate?

What is the lesson it teaches?

How has it impacted you personally?

SAYING #30

What is the saying or teaching?

Who shared the saying or teaching? (mom, dad, grandparents, etc.)

Where did it originate?

What is the lesson it teaches?

How has it impacted you personally?